C000043047

GHOST METHODS

Síofra McSherry is a Northern Irish poet based in London. Her pamphlet *Requiem* was the Poetry Book Society Spring 2020 Pamphlet Choice. Her criticism has been featured in Poetry London, Poetry Wales, this is tomorrow, and the TLS.

Frank Kelleter is a writer and professor of North American cultural history at Freie Universität Berlin, John F. Kennedy Institute. His publications include *Media of Serial Narrative* (2017), *David Bowie* (2016), and *Serial Agencies* (2014).

ISBN: 978-1-915760-98-2

Cover designed by Aaron Kent

Edited & Typeset by Aaron Kent

Broken Sleep Books Ltd
Rhydwen
Talgarreg
Ceredigion
SA44 4HB

Broken Sleep Books Ltd
Fair View
St Georges Road
Cornwall
PL26 7YH

Ghost Methods

Síofra McSherry

Also by Síofra McSherry

Requiem   (The Emma Press, 2020)

CONTENTS

For Sean

Gen moun ki fe sèman yo tande'l ap chante:
Papa Gèdè bel gason
Gèdè Nibo bel gason
Abiye tout an blan, pou l'al monte o palè

Fuck the police

ON SEAN BONNEY

Death is ours. Everybody knows this. But Sean Bonney knew it truly: His final book, *Our Death*, written in Berlin between 2016 and 2019, reads like a fractured prayer. That's easy to say, with that title, but how can you read these last poems and not think suicide note. One even contains a testament, Sean giving away the weird treasures of his life to friends and enemies. The poem, "From Deep Darkness," ends in heartbreak: "I love you all so fucking much."

He wrote about his friends a lot. Now all that his friends can do is write about him. Or to him. Address him as if he was still here. Sean. Are you okay?

Other poems, the ones he's probably best known for, are contemptuous, unforgiving, brutal. Terrorist poems slashing Tory throats. How can so sweet a man hold so much hatred? But then you saw him perform and understood. He spat at law enforcement, railed against the firmament. The FIRMAMENT. I want to say: Let that sink in. But this is not an expression he would have used. I've never seen someone so sickened by clichés and yet he understood them like Fassbinder understood *schlager* music. The painful hope that's confined in false words and false gestures. Rereading Sean's books and pamphlets now, from the forbidding experimentalism of *Blade Pitch Control Unit*, *The Commons* and *Happiness* to the bitterness of *Letters against the Firmament* to the dark sincerity of *Ghosts* and *Our Death*, I think he was searching for a language of true intimacy: a language that can never be taken away from us, not ever turned against us.

Us? Perhaps another cliché, but one that rises from deep sources of affection. You should have heard him talk about the people he loved. He was fiercely protective of his friends, their transitions made him tremble with fear and care. Always worried about people's bodies too. What goes in and out. Evil substances and kind words.

Sean was a political poet because he knew which strange powers can seize a body. As an epileptic, he was viscerally acquainted with unholy, fascist gods. One of his most frightful poems is about a dead man lying on the pavement at Kottbusser Tor, head smashed open, "maybe he'd jumped from his balcony." Sean always dismissed straightforwardly biographical readings but this had happened to him. It was as if he saw himself lying there. As if he foresaw himself in his own poem.

How strange that Sean died before a pandemic that seems to have crept into his writing long before it registered anywhere else. When two of his friends meet now, I guess they sooner or later ask themselves how he would write about our present collapses.

I want to say violence and tenderness, because he haunted himself and he was loved for it. He possessed his body like a demon. That's violence. He inhabited his body like a friend. That's tenderness. I don't know what to say about the drugs. No two people are addicted in the same way. I know it made many of us sad. Being asked "Are you okay?" meant the world to him (is what he told me). It meant a life to him.

One night in his vertiginous Kreuzberg apartment, listening to Bowie, we talked about tattoos. He was contemplating a stick and poke "We Are The Dead". Nice, I said, but what if this becomes the title of a successful zombie sitcom? Ugh, he said, I need to spell it "R" then. Some of his best poems respell song lines and titles. Thrash Me, It Hurts to Be Murdered, Black Cocaine, Anywhere Out of the World, Where Have They Been, Under Duress, Let's Not Chat About Despair. Throw a rock against the road and it breaks into pieces. I remember the Xeroxed pictures of famous singers, poets, artists glued to the naked walls of his apartment. Bowie Dylan Fassbinder, suddenly looking like abandoned heroes in abandoned buildings. His Bowie was the angular madman, the tortured distortion artist, who cuts up sentences and sounds so they can be fabulous again. His Dylan was the Dylan of Idiot Wind, the vengeful con artist who wants to turn his back and scream at love because what can you do? It's a wonder we can even feed ourselves. His Fassbinder was the delicate comrade, the beat child, the raging tyrant of desire and devotion. Sean's office at Freie Universität had these pictures too. They made our instituted make-believe world look strangely transitional. He was the friendliest presence in the building, agendaless. So forgiving of our conceits, so generous about his other worlds, a guest, a ghost. We should have sealed his office after he died. Should have kept the bookshelves stacked with anarchist flyers, the walls adorned with Mustapha Khayati Sophie Scholl Amiri Baraka Pier Paolo Pasolini Anita Berber Katerina Gogou Diamanda Gálas. These were his people.

In the first surreal months of the pandemic, I rewatched all Fassbinder films on old pirate DVDs from China with Mandarin subtitles you couldn't turn off. During lockdown, this was a special national nightmare. Like picking German scabs until they bled glamorous patterns. It also felt like Sean was there, in every melodramatic camera angle, every piece of cold or frantic dialogue. Now I'm thinking: Bonney in Berlin – that was the insomniac infiltrator who short-circuited the madness of two pathetic countries, England and Germany, rival business monsters from the same pale hell. His Berlin was not the cool capital of the expatriates, not the poor-but-sexy joke of a slogan. (It wasn't my Berlin of faculty meetings and cocktail bars either.) He didn't want to die in Britain, that's why he left London, didn't want to die in Berlin, I think, but who knows. Athens would have been next, failed Europe's beaten heart, where he found a gorgeous new scene, another underground metropolis. "I'll tell you all about it when I see you," his last text message said.

It didn't happen. No more messages, no more get-togethers. But his friends will keep talking to him. As good as we can. Síofra's *Ghost Methods* is no monologue. Her "Series of Posthumous Discourses with Sean Bonney" reaches out to an absence that is real. I want to say: touching. On the other side of these outraged and beautiful death poems, he is there.

Frank Kelleter
Berlin, 2022

A SERIES OF POSTHUMOUS DISCOURSES
WITH SEAN BONNEY

I. *4 am poem for Sean*

Bonney is fucking dead and there's something twisting and needling in my chest trying to get out and it can't but I can hear your voice going just write a fucking poem about it mate and I mean fair enough, yeah. Bodies are agents of the state. Being in a body is like sticking a cat in a rucksack, it's uncomfortable and dangerous and it's temporary. Bodies are prone to the consumption of massive amounts of amphetamines. Bodies are like poems are like Tudor houses with snake-eyed priests jammed into all the cubbyholes ready to take you down in the final reel (cops more like, you'd say. Same difference, I say). Bodies fucking die and that is not a fucking metaphor. It's 3.30 am on I forget what day and London and Berlin and Athens have been burning out the stars for you all night and if any of these fickle suns ever rise again above Kreuzberg it will be over an altar all covered in ash. Wait a second, what movie is this again, is it the one where the mirrors have stolen all the words and we're all just mouthing at each other like a telly with the sound off and the pale inside priests are busy hacking their way outwards to the skin with their long nails that are actually blades that are actually, you know, self-loathing or whatever psychic downer our subconscious vomited up today from the pits of the human condition. "Dylan is good," you used to say, ignoring the bloody priest fingernails sticking out all over us and waving. "He's not," I would say, I don't know why. He's better than fingerknives. This is not a Sean Bonney poem. That pulse you had, Jesus, that was something, you set words off like a rocket. Like a brick at Nazis. You better be haunting the fuck out of the means of production. You better be chortling away up there at something Mark Fisher said over a pint. Sun Ra had better be playing. Anyway it's 4 am and there are no words left because you had the words, you had all of them, and you're fucking gone mate.

2. *Conversation with the ghost of SB*

Well old friend
neither locks nor fleshy inconvenience hold you now

you can slip between police lines
between the ground and the protester's face
into the cracks in the walls of the flats we're priced out of
into the cold itchy beds of the comfortless

or here I guess
I welcome your transparent interruptions
you may peep and glimmer away

I have been a champion of the incarnate condition
but current miseries challenge my best efforts

we're all moving further and further apart

from a posthumous perspective have you any
experience to bring to bear on the matter
could you smear some of your phantomish knowing
on this softly unbearable situation

I don't know if you've been following the news
noli me tangere cry the uninfected
as their edges start to glow like ectoplasm

in Bergamo the corpse of our sister weeps
into the clingfilm we have wrapped her in

listen can you hear the silence
creeping through the concert halls
it's the poor and old struggling to breathe

what have the dead to say to the living
as we try to keep our weak this way

—*let the ghosts touch*
—*let the ghosts touch*
—*let the ghosts touch*

3. *Berlin, November*

I was just sitting here thinking about you
and how from a certain perspective society is nothing but the interaction of
planes of power
although that's the kind of perspective that can kill us and in particular you
and I was wondering which of the spirits of the dead appeared to you as you
lay there
breaking down the borders inside your body in a cascading revolution
against the material conditions of being alive
and what secrets they let you in on considering you were close to a spirit yourself
you were a fine-boned ear pricked to the hum of the other world

I imagine them clustering round you, or settling, perhaps
I like to think of the dead gently sinking down on top of each other as in
the formation of sedimentary rock
piled on one another and on you until you are covered in soft dead like snow

Down here we are still debating how many cops you can balance on the
head of a pin
and the horrible technologies of the master's house
I wonder if there are ghost cops and ghost fascists and sickeningly brutal
ghost methods
of annihilating resistance to the concept that what *is*
has been since the beginning and ever shall be
and that the act of imagining a world where things are otherwise, where
things are okay,
where we're all looked after is anything other than sacred, utter observance

I hope not
I hope it's light and loose where you are
I hope music is something you can hold
Berlin is PTSD
It's a conversation overheard between a junkie and a haunted doll that
appears in the corner of his room at night
What does it fucking want
The city has a bombsite texture
like breathing air that just now had a scream in it

I always knew which of my lovers would be the first to die
Our soft bodies draw all the pain in a place towards themselves
Little sensate pots of nerve endings that we are
Little polyps, little sea urchins
So squeezable! So crushable!
Living can leave such lacerations
You were the only sane one of us

4. *Sticking around*

It's not the leaving, it's the staying gone
Daylight returns every morning for another encore
I've been in my right mind for ninety-two

Twitter says, learn to say no to things that stand in the way of life

like the demons on an everlasting smoke break outside my back door
They smile like sharks, but the conversation really flows
You may abandon hope, they chuckle, *but we'll never abandon you!*

like the wall in my apartment that grew a soft coat of mould each winter
that I poisoned and painted over again and again

like surrendering to the horror of what we are:
bags of flesh and bone set in motion by sluices and sparks,
subject to the psychosis of consciousness

like two hundred milligrams of diacetylmorphine and twenty-two Valiums
Is that a lot? I asked, also, *what is it like?*
Bliss, you said, *sunrise on Venus, an orgasm in the blood*
Five days you were gone that time

(It wasn't the leaving, though, was it, it was the staying gone
because by god, the dead have plenty to say
and they're everywhere, whittering away like sparrows)

like—refusing to listen to the chattering dead

Put away that Ouija board, go haunt your own house

Twitter says, learn to say yes to things that support life

like my girl M. tattooing her own arm with a needle
No-one was more present than she was then
stitched to the indelible now

like using "cunt" in a poem, then taking it out
then putting it back when you said I was being silly

like I'm sorry, this is beyond me, you need professional help
in a voice as gentle as my cat's tongue on my wrist

like my neighbour playing *The Piano* by Michael Nyman as I lay here
every day for two months until she could do it without mistakes
I'm proud of her

Listen, you naysayers, you sibilant haunts,
I've read Fred Moten; I know sitting in the sunlight on this patch of grass
or rubbing this tattoo that reminds me of LA or eating strawberries until
I'm sick
or playing some banger by The Fall over and over is not decolonial praxis

but adrienne maree brown says if we refuse to settle for suffering
pleasure can be radical, and shouldn't freedom feel like bliss?
Though it's nothing to smack, I'm sure

Sorry, that came off kind of bitter
I'm just tired of losing mentors, friends I loved

I'm aware the joys of my white body won't make up for the innumerable
hair fractures suffered by the heart, nor capitalism
but your meandering deaths were no help either

I know what it is to see monsters in the sky
the wasteland of our colonial inheritance spread out
as far as the eye can see dotted with charred and bloody piles

I too am veined through with vision that grasps for words
I've taken a running jump past sanity

and I am here, I am here, I am still here
filling this page with lines that maybe someone somewhere will read
and know that even so you can hunker down if you want to
you can write and (same thing) survive

ZONBI

The eyelids of the night are closed above
the turning eyeball of the blinded earth.
All is dark, and you can hear no sound.
You can't recall how you came to be here.
You're both alive and dead, or maybe neither—
eyes and ears prove nothing either way.
There are creatures that fare better in the dark,
those with use of echo, whisker, scent,
but all you have's yourself, curled like a foetus
or a sleeping snake. You lie on earth
that's cold as a grave and open to the sky.
Maybe you're with the ancestors already,
last in a long parade of Ulster folk
in stone houses, sparing of heat and light,
speaking little, saying less, bending
iron to their will before the forge.
You don't feel like an ancestor, but then
you can't imagine any of them do.
Even the ceaseless dead start at day one.
Still, best perhaps to proceed like you're alive.
Turning to stare up into endless night
you spot the light of a single, quiet star.
Darkness may be immanent, and follow
fast on the heels of all extinguishings,
but look, recall the ancientness of light!
The star, too, may be dead by now. No matter.
Light requires no reason to go on,
so why should you? Get up from the ground,
take one step, then the next. Start with the star.

HAMLET V:1

There'll be no rest here until we're dead.
The play is yet afoot, and we are bound
to entertain, to hold up the death's-head.
The clowns jump back up from the ground.
I guess people can get used to anything;
these days we sing at our grave-making.

The play is yet afoot, and we are bound
to stay and see things out, and at the end
quietly depart as the curtain's downed.
Often folks are tempted to extend
their time onstage by fair means and by foul.
Everything from alchemy to make-up by the trowel

is entertained to hold up the death's-head.
The modern mage has given up witchcraft
pursuing the immortal through technology instead.
This is a design for life by Lovecraft.
Silicon has gotten in the bloodstream;
the future is frozen, or a digital dream.

The clowns jump back up from the ground.
They patiently explain to the gloomy Dane
that graves are for the dead. They've always found
the abstractions of the rich to be vain
and troubling. Look at the prince, addressing a brainless
bone as if the dead thing were a person. Heinous.

I guess people can get used to anything,
perhaps even knowing that we'll die.
Imagine, your precious mind, the wellspring
of what you call *yourself*, will putrefy.
Just a hollow stinking braincase will remain—
mute, but resolute—to rebuke the Dane.

These days we sing at our grave-making;
we've thrown in our lot with Yorick. André
Tchaikovsky left his head to the RSC, stating
he'd like the Company to use it in the play.
They boiled and bleached it, and they do.
It grins at David Tennant. Soon we will, too.

A DISCOURSE

Me, the poet, as herself: I am an ocean. I am a frothing pot of molecules slipping one over the other. Direction is meaningless and I breathe condensed gravity

Her, the poet, enraptured by knowledge of the manifest divine: *silence*

Me: Where is my albatross? Where is my lighthouse, my first sight of land?

Her: *breaking up* .- ... . / - - --- / .- ... .

Me: I don't understand.

Her: Soft to soft remaining—flakes after fire—

Me: Come again

Her: Summat bitter, and entrails in-mixed. Under and in.

Me: Mouthing and blether. I am drowning. Help.

Her: *coughing and spitting sounds*

Me: …

Her: *booming* What is a drop of water to the sea?

Me: All. Nothing. Neither know of themselves. Lost

Her: On the contrary. It is sought no further

Me: Lost and found are a matter of perspective

Her: Do you know what you were before ocean

Me: Fir and moss. Dappled and susurrus. Fronds dip and rustle. A coppiced cathedral

Her: You remember the soft things tight in the roots

Me: Yes and the throats of birds inflated with song and the green world englobed in the convex eye of a deer

Her: You remember the forest

Me: Yes

Her: The forest is ash

Me: It is ocean season

Her: Yes

SOME TIME LATER

Her: *to me*

      Wake up a guest is with us

The guest, everything that's left, the outside of things: I wish to know you

Me: For what reason

The guest: I have understood all that has been and ever will. The earth whispers its secrets in my ear. All the seas and skies are known to me. I do not know you

Me: …

The guest: Why do you not respond

Me: *with a shrug*

It is ocean season. The wash of the wave and

Her: *interrupting*

We are the air. Whip me up into your hurricanes. I have felt you pass a million times

The guest: What of it

Her: My anger shines in your eyes and your face struggles to find expression

Why do you not respond

You stumble through the ashes of your dreams

I ask why you are not screaming

KORSÖRER STRASSE

for Mathilde

Spring held its breath until the cherries bloomed pink,
crowning your quiet street with perfumed pink.

At first just a few hundred blossoms opened,
but in two weeks the trees were all costumed pink.

Every day crowds came to see the cherry trees;
they touched and crushed and consumed pink.

Girls came in sundresses bursting with summer.
Brides posed in front of the doomed pink.

As the blossoms died in a steady, silent rain,
we dreamed in waves that spumed pink.

You cried in my arms over what you had lost.
I spoke of coming cherries, enwombed, pink.

Cherie, the fruits now sweet on your tongue
are bloody with the past, wound-pink.

PEOPLE MAKE MISTAKES ALL THE TIME

A A

A O

Something in my mother was stubborn as a squatting toad and I admire that, I do especially now she has been so long in the soil

That belligerent amphibian met something it couldn't stare down – but I have covered this elsewhere, the point is she held fast against other folks' realities particularly mine. My dress size was 14 when it was actually 8 the bats in the back garden were just swallows wagging their wings like they'd been snapped and my blood type could not be O

A B

A B AB O

The red puddle

of courage

A AB

A B AB

Press your palms over your shell-likes and listen to the rush of your own blood the echo and chatter, the seagull and wave of the underground sea within us all

27

A O

an ocean which, fingers crossed, will never see the light
beyond a pinprick here and there and not too often
But beware, the dark will drown you fast
as a choleric Venetian summer heavy with reverie
the obsession with not-life, the trance of being not here but inside

A O

For eighteen months of this brief life I had a needlebite mark
below the elbow almost all the time where my blood
came out into tubes, and once as a fountain
when in confusion I pulled the drip line from my arm
They bound it up in a red that matched the floor and wall
I didn't trust the doctors I said, *but…what do doctors do?* he said
They bleed you and bleed you until you're dead

B B

B O

Lucy Westenra probably died from the multiple transfusions
to which the men in her life subjected her, in an effort to restore
what the vampire had taken — it wasn't until blood types were discovered
in 1901 that doctors understood why the procedure failed so often

28

and *Dracula* came out in 1897. She was a whore, anyway, the redhead
with all their blood inside her, and besides when the vampire came she liked it
Not like Mina Harker, scarred and agonised. Mina had to love him, first

B O   B O

I donate blood sometimes, and you should too if possible
(isn't it grand when poetry makes a difference in the world)
The health service is always after me because I'm O-
the universal donor. They can stick our blood in anyone
so it's carried in ambulances, whereas we can only have our own
I have to wait this time so I read the brochure back to front and there's a chart
with the blood type inheritance groups. *Bloody hell*

B AB   A B AB

The donation centre can't keep their staff, that's why there's a wait today
It's the smell that gets to people, the nurse tells me, the stench
of iron when it spills. *They can't handle it so they leave in a few weeks*
It's true, blood is disgusting. Poor Dracula
We think we're above the earth but at the end of the day
it's iron and salt that comes pouring out of us

and it won't be long before we're mud

AB AB   A B AB

Can you check your blood type for me? I ask him
just to make sure

Red, he replies

AB O   A B

"Trauma and loss are not, in themselves, art: they are like half a metaphor"
some Louise Glück for you there, from her essay on healing
i.e., there's no point just sucking the blood out of a thing, that's no use to anyone
You have to stick it back into someone else, and maybe it helps them
or at least offers the gift of what we continue to call "art"
for want of agreement on a better term. A coarse metaphor, I own,
but I think I earned it

O O   O

WINTER SONG

Today I left the last place I called home,
another intergalactic junkyard I held
a square of space in through will alone,
it felt sometimes, and what might pass for love.
It had a low beam across the centre of the ceiling
I hit my head on daily, and a constant breath of wind
from the badly installed Velux window blew
my cat's fur into corners. She's dead now.

Never mind all that.
My hearths are in my heart.

Joy is what is left once life has been wrung
through the cheesecloths of inexorable change.
Rather, there's joy (the cheese) and the waters of grief.
I have chosen this analogy for its simplicity though I admit
joy is inadequately represented by cottage cheese.
Bear with me. The joy is here, I'm holding (eating?) it,
a crumbly substance with a sourly gentle taste.
The grief runs from me, salty and transparent.

Much of the business of living has to do with
acts of separation, and I like to think I do it well.
Separating, I mean — one thing from the other,
each note from the next, which is a fundamental
challenge of musicianship from your first stumbling
fingerings on guitar to performing coloratura,
which means to sing a run of notes very quickly without
blurring them together. Things are not the same.

Another example: yesterday is not today,
although I jerked awake with the same metallic
flavour in my mouth and the same relentless
winter sun rising over the sea into my bedroom
window frame. Suffice to say these days I would prefer

to be asleep: I am not, so here I am, writing.
This morning my pen curls in praise around a small
green bird outside I do not know the name of.

I grieve the names, the many names
my mouth with never form again.

LANDSCAPE WITH A FALL

For D.

On a summer's day a long time ago
I fell in love with Death.
He killed me.
What did you expect?

The big surprise was that he fell in love with me,
and now he kills a piece of me each day.

Every day I rise again,
a brunette, quotidian revenant
just trying to reach her goals
and self-actualize.

I woke this morning, for example,
to find my right hand gone: my writing hand,
which the little shit knows full well.
Bear with me: I will be typing awkwardly
with just my left until the right grows back.

My fetid suitor finds all this adorable.
He likes to see me rise against his horrors
as though it were an inconvenience, that's all,
to be trapped in a body which decays.

I was just getting used to it, the constant
pourings out and refillings, when I saw you there,
stoic as a lighthouse with your revolving halo
of impenetrable rock and a beer —
the latest of several, you informed me,
regretfully, the next day by email.

My first sight of land was a man
in a mac by the bar, that's all.

Meanwhile I, shot as an albatross,
bled silently in front of you all night
and prayed you were too drunk to notice.

When you left me I was struck down to the bone,
rejecting food, and sleep, and life
as determinedly as a corpse.

Wide-eyed Death hovered helplessly by my side
wondering why I would not resurrect, and where
the wound you'd landed was.
It was exhausting to explain:
Death has no heart, and he could see that mine,
physiologically speaking, was quite well.
It's a human thing, I said.

He looked me in the eyes and saw
another, equal and implacable Force
had given terrible birth there (saw, too,
his own face reflected back, as if for a moment
the sun and moon hung together
in pale late afternoon blue skies),
and with a grin —
he does everything with a grin —
suggested it might help to get away for a few days.

I flew from nowhere to nowhere
weeping the whole way,
gazing out at the ice-white air.
I tangled myself in strange sheets and stared
pointlessly into foreign lakes, searching for the small
sight of love, drowning in the corner
of the picture, unremarkably.

When I got back I tracked you down
and held my hurt out to you with both hands.
Here, take it: it's yours, I said,
and you took that awful gift and held it

as it writhed and tore and bit
and almost overthrew you, although
it could not.

Time spins around a still point:
another bar, another beer, another flight.
Without you I bathe my body first in sun,
then sea, then sun again, letting her freckle
and brown. The laughter of beloved friends
forms chain links in the summer air.

We write, and write.
I send my mails at night,
yours come in the morning, under full sun.
I lie back and hold up the phone
and let your words fall on me in place of you.

Meanwhile, offshore, in a splash of white
foam against the verdigris sea,
Death quietly drowns.

ACKNOWLEDGEMENTS

All my love and gratitude to Martin Clarke and Greg Reisman, who gave me back the conditions of life, and to Kevin Winter, Malcolm Cocks, Nia Davies, Tom McLaughlin, and Daniel McShane for being, endlessly, relentlessly there. Many thanks to Alice Oswald, Nadira Wallace, Susy Lansman, Declan Ryan, and Tristram Fane Saunders for thoughtful feedback, to Sean, for the haunting, and Haiti, although she is a cat and deceased, and wouldn't care anyway.

"Conversation with the ghost of SB" appeared in the *Write Where We Are Now* project in April 2020

"Berlin, November" appeared in *Streetcake* magazine in June 2020

"Korsörer Strasse" appeared in *Anthropocene* in January 2023

For 'lay out your unrest' say fuck the police

Lightning Source UK Ltd.
Milton Keynes UK
UKHW010656090223
416681UK00007B/1882

9 781915 760982